Tom Reed

85

The

Granite Avatars

of

Patagonia

Photographs and Text
by
Tom Reed

Forward to the Photographs
by
Dr. Shozo Sato

Published by
Wild Coast Media
P O Box 1451, Fort Bragg, California 95437

The text of this book is a modified excerpt
from a larger work entitled *The Other Side*

Book and cover designed by Tom Reed
First Edition 2009

Quote on page 84 © Krishnamurti Foundation of America, by permission

ISBN 978-0-9816997-5-2

Library of Congress Control Number: 2008936437

Organizations may obtain quantity discounts on bulk purchases of this book
for gift purposes, or as premiums for increasing membership or subscriptions. Please contact the publisher

Original Photographic Prints
of all of the black and white images in this book
are available to purchase from
www.tomreed.com

Acknowledgements

I would not have undertaken this project without the encouragement from Dr Shozo Sato, who appreciated my photographs, and from Irene D. Thomas, who appreciated my writing. Both of them have taught me in the course of creating this book. Dr. Sato never tires of teaching me how to locate my "chop" (red stamp)--an art that I am slow to learn--and Irene has been a good editor, never tiring of teaching me how to use a semicolon--another art that eludes me. Valuable input from readers, especially Liz Collins and Asia Freeman, was essential to refining the text. You all have my deepest gratitude

The project cannot succeed without the support of those who purchase this first printing, and to you I also extend my sincere gratitude in advance.

Preface

My first encounter with the Granite Avatars was in January of 2006. Experiences of my second trip, in March of 2007, were stitched together with the first and written as one journey. Almost every detail is true, but a few things have been massaged to merge the two trips into one or to omit the need for lengthy explanation. Because I lost my camera and all of the 600 photographs taken on the second trip, a third trip was necessary. I returned in January of 2008 for the majority of the photographs on these pages.

All Photographs were taken with compact, lightweight, "point-and-shoot" cameras. All compositions are natural--nothing ever added, nothing removed. *Photoshop* is my digital darkroom. Almost all of the 35 color wildflower photos were taken in the mountains at the base of the avatars, a few were taken nearby in Chile.

2008

Forward to the Photographs

Monochrome landscape photography is very similar to the ancient art of black ink painting, or sumi-e, of China and Japan. The major difference is that the sumi-e artist, after many years of training, uses his years of experience in sketching and painting to intuitively create his work, basing the composition on the use of dominant, sub-dominant and subordinate positions for the subject matter. On the other hand, a photographer must use his trained eye to position himself in such a location where the view allows such a composition, and most importantly, he must then have the patience to wait for the right moment, when the conditions of light, shadows and clouds provide a composition, and then capture that moment. With patience and sharp awareness of the subject matter, a photographer can step beyond ordinary landscape photographs, and create extraordinary ones.

In Japanese art, especially, active empty space is a very important element in the composition. Active empty space in sumi-e is prepared during the process of composing the painting. This active empty space is the place where the viewer of the painting and its creator, the artist, communicate. It is easier for the painter to create such space, because he begins with a blank white space. On the other hand, for a photographer viewing a scene of great nature through the lens of a camera, in which every element of nature is in the composition, a problem arises--the problem of how to create active empty space. Tom Reed often solves this problem by including rich, black shadows, brilliant white snow, or clear sky in his compositions.

Mr. Reed decided to use a *chop*, a seal used in a traditional Japanese painting, as a signature for his monochrome photographs. But finding the right space to place a red seal in a monochrome scene is often a challenge. Sometimes when there is a dead empty space in a composition, that seal can make the space become active and provide a "finishing touch" for a photographic composition.

Tom Reed studied both calligraphy and sumi-e and uses this experience for his creative energy in his photographic images, and I feel he has successfully captured their full beauty.

Dr. Shozo Sato
Professor Emeritus in Japanese Aesthetics;
University of Illinois: Urbana-Champaign Campus.

The
Granite Avatars
of
Patagonia

By Tom Reed

The Bus

My heart and my buttocks had an argument, and my heart won, so I'm twenty-four hours into the thirty-two hours of busses that will deliver me to the tiny town of El Chaltén, at forty-nine degrees south latitude in the Andes of Argentina.

Last year a friend was in Buenos Aires to study tango. While in Argentina she made a few trips, one to the mountain resort of Bariloche, where she bought some postcards with photos of the dramatic granite spires far to the south. She gave me those as a gift, and I taped them to the side of a tall file cabinet beside my desk among clipped photos of other rugged peaks. Over the last year, I've gained inspiration by looking at those postcards. The granite peaks are the most spectacular I've ever seen, and now I'm on my way to stand below them. I don't know it yet, but I'm on a pilgrimage.

A deep yearning in my heart demanded that my posterior endure the bus rides south from Bariloche. I had come to South America to explore the open spaces I saw on maps of coastal Chile, where I imagined forested hills meeting pristine beaches, but after seeing that all those forests had been razed and replaced by monoculture tree plantations of Douglas fir and eucalyptus, I drifted into the wilds of the Andes with those postcard photos a semi-conscious but driving force. After some exciting backpacking trips in Argentina's Nahuel Huapi National Park, I realized I would not be satiated by any mountain but those on the postcards.

So far it's been an uneventful ride across the endless pampas, down the Atlantic coast to the port city of Rio Gallegos. I've been listening to music on my iPod and searching for wildlife. All I've seen so far was a flock of parrots—actually the austral parakeet, but so large anyone but an ornithologist would call them parrots. It's been a lot of staring out the window at arid grassland. I'm just leaving Rio Gallegos, listening to my reggae playlist—"Jah Can Do It," one of my favorites by Dennis Brown. I'm on to Rico Rodriguez's "Fu Man Chu" when a flock of rheas appears out the window. I've been across almost a thousand miles of pampas without sighting a single one and now I feel the thrill of seeing these large flightless birds in the wild. They stand about four feet tall, and keep together in a flock as they flee from the bus. When we pass a scarlet-breasted bird standing on a fence post, I consult my field guide and guess that it's a long-tailed meadowlark. Only a few minutes later there's another flock of rheas, and they're huge. I assume the birds in the first flock were all immature, as several adults in this flock stand six feet tall, but then I realize it is possible, and I would guess likely, that they are two different species. The greater rhea is not supposed to be this far south, but there it is right outside the window—I see six-foot tall birds—so the smaller ones may be the lesser rhea, which is supposed to inhabit these southern pampas. They run across the pampas, frightened by the bus. I'm tapping people on the shoulder to get them to look out the windows, wondering what it would be like to be out there on the ground with them as they charge across the grassland. The image reminds me of the scene early in the film "Jurassic Park" in which the ostrich-like dinosaurs stampede by the humans. Rhea males impregnate several females who all contribute eggs to his nest, which he defends while he incubates them. During this time he can be aggressive in his defense of the clutch, and the sharp claws of a man-sized cock charging at thirty-five miles-per-hour is close enough to Jurassic Park that I would be sure to avoid them in spring.

Not long afterwards I see my first herd of wild guanacos. These are large camelids with golden backs and white sides and bellies. They stand still in groups of eight to twelve. The guanaco population has decreased from a half-billion before the Europeans arrived, to a half-million today, so the indigenous people must not have hunted them seriously, at least not successfully. The long necks of these and the rheas makes me incorrectly assume that the aboriginal choice of hunting weapon, the *bola*, was used to strangle both of these animals whose necks offer such a large target. But actually the bola was thrown at the legs to "hog tie" them. I guess that's why Gauchos learned how to use bolas from the Indians. The Patagonian bola was made of two or three braided leather cords, each with a small leather sack filled with pebbles or a wooden ball at the ends of the cords. Gauchos would use them on cattle back in the day.

Later the clouds seem to drop down on us. They are cirrus and nimbus—clouds of high elevation—but they are only a few hundred feet above. It is quite surreal, as if the sky doesn't fit the landscape.

Each time we cross an occasional slough I'm alert to see any wildlife that may visit for the water. There's a big goose at one, but I'm not even sure if it's wild, as these sloughs also attract homesteaders, and a little farmhouse is nearby. At times the road-side is thick with daisy-like wildflowers. A healthy carancho—what looks like a cross between a goshawk and a raven, but is actually in the falcon family—tops a fencepost and watches us pass. At a road-cut the exposed subterranean cobbles reveal that this place was once underwater. Blue mountains serrate the western horizon.

Some impressive vertical walls stand in the distance. As we approach El Calafate I realize that we have indeed gained high elevation, having climbed very gradually on a seemingly flat, but tilted, landscape. When we descend a steep canyon wall into a big valley that holds Lago Argentino my ears pop. We roll slowly in low gear to keep the brakes cool. While looking out the window on the other side of the bus I realize that the young guy sitting next to the window resembles my older brother when he was the same age—about twenty-one. He also has a wife and two-year-old son, as my brother did then. I consider asking him for his photograph, but decide not to, feeling awkward.

We arrive in El Calafate—named for a thorny blueberry that grows in the area. It's a bit of a boomtown, filled with young tourists carrying backpacks. Obviously the place has recently become a Mecca for them because of the nearby glacier, but the locals are doing a good job of developing in a consistent rustic mountain theme. The town sits on the south shore of the huge lake. Eager to get into the mountains, from the bus I march directly to the counter to buy a ticket to El Chaltén, four hours to the north, and succeed. In my thirty-minute layover, I find a grocery store and buy bread, cheese and olive loaf cold cuts, then sit on the curb of the terminal parking lot where I can keep an eye on my bus—a habit I've developed over the years—and make a few sandwiches.

Heading out of town, we pass a glacial erratic the size of a house. It probably fell to the bottom of an ancient glacial lake when the iceberg that carried it melted. Something white is on the other side of the lake, and I'd bet it's an iceberg. After about twenty minutes of back-tracking eastward on the single road into town, we hang a left, and leave the pavement, heading north along the eastern shore of the lake, crossing a tur-quoise river, the Santa Cruz, which drains it to the Atlantic. The silvery lake shimmers in the late afternoon sun west of an expanse of sand dunes. Beyond the lake are the Andes, obscured by dark purple rainstorms broken only by sporadic shafts of light. Then we cross another river, this one flowing *into* the lake. The geography is unusual. The next lake to the north, Lago Viedma, is of an equal size as this Lago Argentino. The two lakes are obvi-ously the drowned valleys of huge glaciers from another epoch. They run parallel, from west to east, separated by twenty-five miles of mountains, but the river that drains Lago Viedma, Rio la Leona, runs south through a gap in the foothills of the mountains instead of spilling out onto the pampas as a normal river would. It must have been diverted by a massive terminal moraine at the end of the last ice age. This river dumps into Lago Ar-gentino just a couple miles north of the origin of the Santa Cruz, probably doubling that river's size. I wonder what it would be like to run that river across the pampas to the At-lantic—would there be whitewater, wildlife? The map shows only one little bridge between the lake and the ocean, 140 miles as the crow flies, maybe 200 on the water. We follow Rio la Leona to the north. I see those grey geese again. They must be wild, but I don't see them in my bird book. Elephant toe formations of sandstone remind me of California desert excursions I've made. The badlands east of Borrego Springs come to mind. Frisbee-shaped lenticular clouds are stacked six-high to the north, like a squadron of UFO's coming in for a landing. Junco-like birds called negritos fly from bush to bush.

We exit the mountains and pass the entire east shore of the Lago Viedma, then turn left at a *cruz*, as an intersection is called, and head up the north shore for the mountains. The drive takes some time; my excitement, anticipating views of the peaks, probably makes it seem longer than it is. About twenty miles from El Chaltén we pass a shallow pond where I see a large flock of Chilean Flamingos. Though my book told me that they range all over the southern cone, I still find it bizarre to see them out the side window, and turn my head to see glaciers and peaks dusted with fresh snow out the front window. I'm at forty-nine degrees of latitude. It's the equivalent of seeing flamingoes in the sloughs of Sas-katchewan. Cottontail rabbits, introduced from Europe, run across the road, just as they do up north, in a way that is enough to make one question Darwin.

They are well-hidden in the brush beside the road, but when a vehicle passes, they choose to run across the road in front of the vehicle. One may argue that they evolved without the input of vehicles, but it's my guess that they would do the same if spooked by a predator. I could never understand how this helps them to "further their genes." One of them doubts its decision to cross the road, and stops. The bus runs right over it. If it remained motionless it survived, with the big bus wheels racing by on both sides. A pair of Andean foxes wanders across the road ahead, and the driver leans on the horn. They split up, one to each side of the road. They're a more squat, dog-looking animal than our sleek foxes of the north, but colored similar to our grey fox.

We arrive after sunset, at about 10:30, and my guess is that there'll be no room at the inn, whichever one I choose, and I'm right. So I hang out at the bar in the big dining room of a busy hostel at the far end of town, closest to the mountains, drink a liter of Quilmes and chat with a few folks before wandering off into the blackness after midnight to find the area where free camping is allowed.

The road is unscreened gravel, and I occasionally roll my ankle on an oversized cobble that I can't see without the light of a moon or stars. But I do find a sign for free camping, and it directs me down a steep slope, and under a barbed wire fence. Inside there is a tent village. I raise mine in a space by the fence in a light gusty rain. As I crawl in, it begins coming down with force. The tall grass makes a great bed, better than any hostel, and I sleep like a baby, or as a baby should, all night.

In the morning the weather remains: wind and rain. But after a while the rain lightens and the sun peeks out from time to time. The wind is a warm williwaw descending from the continental divide where it lets its water content go, gaining the latent energy of that water's previous evaporation, in the form of heat. It feels funny. I don't like it. I'm sure it's full of positive ions. I wonder where this water falling on me was when it evaporated. Probably the South Pacific, but maybe a glacier in New Zealand. As I walk across town, waves of dust rise from the road, blowing in the eyes of hikers headed for the trailhead behind me. The big granite peaks are obscured by clouds driven by an angry wind. I duck into a café for tea and ham empanadas, then visit the park visitor's center to register for the backcountry and get an "official" map showing only the "official" trails. Already I can tell from their layout that I will be spending most of my time off of those, as they mostly radiate from town on routes needed by day-hikers.

A girl at the Patagonia Hostel gives me some good information and sells me a fairly good map. It has the "unofficial" trails that will take me where I want to go without back-tracking. She recommends that I camp at "El Refugio," on the bank of the river, so I move camp there, where the aging hippie owner tells me they have a hot shower, and most importantly, they will guard my street gear while I'm in the mountains. It's only ten pesos a day—just over three dollars. As I pitch my tent a flock of parakeets passes close by, chattering excitedly as if they are happy to see me. If they are, the feeling is mutual.

I shop for a bit more food and find salami and bread, both sold by the 100-gram weight, then stop in a "Cerveza Artisana," a microbrew pub, and have a slightly green bock beer, which I appreciate more for its uniqueness than its flavor, in a crowded little rustic cabin. Nearby there's an interesting restaurant with a side of lamb cooking in the front window and a sign reading, "La Casita." There I enjoy an excellent steak with mashed potatoes and a copa de vino tinto. I tried being a vegetarian for eight years, but after I weakened, three acupuncturists all convinced me to eat meat again. My body needs it, and this grass-fed beef in Argentina is as healthy as it gets.

The Two Towers

At dawn, frost covers the grass, sparkling in a wintery way. After breaking camp, I cull all the stuff that I won't need from my pack. It's travel stuff, not needed on the trail. I stash a box of it in the office, and ask for the trailhead. The old hippie, reeking of tobacco, even at this hour, tells me, "It's right there," and points across the street. I follow his finger, but the side-street dead-ends with no trail. So I climb a fence and get on a dirt road, and go west at a fork. At a second fork I see a trail up on the slope to the right, and a building on the left, so I decide to go right. That way bends left and takes me to the building, some sort of recreational clubhouse, behind which I find the trailhead. The route climbs through an Oregon Desert landscape, with big round reddish boulders and outcroppings that would serve well as an ambush scene in an old western movie.

2008

The trail makes a steady but easy climb. Eventually I get to a viewpoint and see the spectacular Cerro Torre for the first time, in the distance, up a glacial valley and below a waning moon. El Torre, "The Tower" is a spike of granite thrusting about 5000 feet up from the side of a glacier. A thrill buzzes through my body in anticipation of what views lie ahead, but I stop here for a bread-and-cheese breakfast, and watch finches and flickers flying by. A packer passes me with two loaded horses behind his own, all in a trot. He's

got a mustache and a black beret. His feet fit into foot-holes, above five-pointed stars, in the tops of big iron discs that are his stirrups. I follow him through an enchanted lenga, (or southern beech) forest. It looks more Japanese than any forest I've seen in Japan. The horizontal layers of foliage, leaves that only grow up, and the sixty-degree branching pattern all make these trees look sculpted by gardeners from a Zen temple. Out of the forest I cross a gravel floodplain, and climb over an old terminal moraine before finding the camp, which is full of tents. I pass through the whole thing and take the westernmost, windward-most site, pitch my tent, and sit in the sun with lunch. A guy walks by and asks in Spanish if there is a bridge across the river. I hear his English accent and tell him I don't know, I just got here, in our shared language, so he continues on.

I pack up for a hike and head to the terminal lake. There the view across the lake is more than outstanding. Cerro Torre dominates the landscape as if the entire valley was constructed with that in mind. I don't think I've ever seen anything this powerful. It is truly majestic, standing 3100 meters tall (I am below 1000). The main tower has two sheer walls of smooth granite as seen from the lake. Various ledges hold impressively thick beds of ice. The pinnacle's west side and top are caked with rime ice that I imagine is plastered there by the severe and near constant attack of the wind carrying vapor from the South Pacific across the Chilean icefield. As that wind meets the tower I think it gets compressed and shoots upward under pressure. At the peak, that pressure is released and the vapor instantly condenses and freezes, building a bulb of airy ice on the west side of the summit. The tower rises from a jagged, snow-covered ridge running up from the south called the "Cordon Adela," and after the main tower, drops off in a series of lesser towers, the most prominent bearing the name "Torre Egger," named for Toni Egger who was half of the team that may have first scaled Cerro Torre in 1959. He was lost in an avalanche

on the way down and his camera containing the proof of their making the summit went with him.

Not long ago a person could say such a sight is "Awesome." These days that word has been hijacked and rendered impotent. The young cashier at the local market in California tells me it's awesome when I give him exact change. This state I am now in, however—the state of awe—is anything but weak. It could be the most powerful emotion I know. It's so powerful it wipes other emotions away, and has the potential to wipe the perceived owner of the emotions away too. The majesty may bring one to his knees, the glory may cause one to raise arms as if to scream hallelujah. In my case, I am stunned and stilled. It's a spiritual experience, not different from what I imagine it would be like to see God. My eyes receive the light of the spectacle before me and the image seems to course through my tissues as if to re-educate me viscerally. Each cell of me now knows what Nature is capable of creating—a sculpture of proportions beyond my imagination. The grandeur has literally blown my mind. The radiation of splendor has incinerated my ego.

How can a rock do this to a man? Or maybe the question is "Why?" It seems plausible that man would evolve to perceive his environment as beautiful. This would afford him a sense of ease and comfort that would promote health. But what advantage is there for us to be stricken by awe at the sight of a granite tower? It seems like it would only distract an evolving man from conducting the business of survival, and the ability to survive is an ace in the game of furthering genes. Thoughts of my place in society, the role I play and its rewards, are of no concern in this wonderstruck moment. In fact, it is plainly clear that they are unimportant. What is important is the vista before me, for it instills a clear awareness free of egoic noise, and in this awareness I find my true self, and an uncontrollable smile. I like the Spanish word for smile, *sonrisa*, because it reminds me of "sunrise." That is the nature of this smile—fresh and radiant. It's like a divine joke has been played on me—like the planet gave me a surprise party. My deepest spiritual experiences have always been like that—humorous—because when you see the Truth, everything else that has been occupying your attention seems hilariously silly.

This experience of awe can only be of use to an organism if there is a spiritual dimension to evolution. Is it by the intention of some omnipresent intelligence that man can

experience such ecstasy simply by viewing a huge spike of eroded rock? Or is it by acci-
dent—an unproductive and therefore doomed idiosyncrasy of evolution?

Joseph Campbell said, "We are the eyes of the earth, we are the ears of the earth. What else?" Others propose that we are creation's way of experiencing itself, or God's way of experiencing his creation. Of course, I have no way of knowing if there is a God or a Creator, or a Divine Intelligence. But experiences like this give weight to the theory that we are spiritual beings  having a physical experience, because I see no use for a physical being to have a spiritual experience. The only possible explana- tion for the latter would be mental illness. In my view, it is those who are numb to the magnificence of Na- ture who are insane. Maybe there is one possible explanation to my question: that the experience of awe leads to a reverence for creation that has evolutionary value in that this reverence may provide a means for the survival of a species with the ability to destroy the planet—its own habitat. The reverence would lead to a view of Nature as sacred, and the destruction of Nature as sacrilege. Again, those irreverent must be insane. But all this would imply intentional evolution, since man has not had the ability to disrupt the planetary ecosystem until recently, evolution would have had to be thinking ahead. If Awe by Nature is an emotion evolved to prevent environ- mental destruction, it seems like a failing strategy at this point in time, since we seem to be well on the way to using our destructive ability. This then raises the question, "Can that which drives evolution by intention fail?" Or the better question might be, "Is failure— severe environmental destruction—built into the evolutionary plan as way to facilitate ac- celerated change?" It could be that the experience of awe by Nature is a new development for modern man, but that also seems to imply an intention, because those most successful at furthering their genes in recent centuries have not been environmentalists and Nature- lovers, have they? The questions are numerous and unanswerable, but interesting to consider.

Over the years I've joked about national parks and monuments being a collection of freak vertical landscapes. We love the sheer rock walls of the Yosemite, Zion, and Can- yonlands valleys. We gasp at the tall, sculpted buttes of the Grand Canyon and Monument Valley, and the exposed volcanic necks of Shiprock and Devil's Tower, wonder at the height of the Redwoods, of Denali, and several other tall peaks. The phenomenon might best be

2008

revealed by the bizarre totems of the hoodoos that are the only reason for Bryce Canyon National Park to exist. They are vertical oddities. If they were lying on the ground, there would be no park.

A psychologist might point to the church steeple to explain why we hold a reverence for the vertical. It points to heaven—to God. I'm not so sure. It could be that the vertical landscapes make us feel small. Some find that amusing: "Wow, it's so big!" Others find it stunning: "Wow, I'm so tiny!" The latter are those whose continuum of ego may be fractured, allowing a moment of profound peace to open the heart.

A woman is sitting on a rock at the edge of the lake with a faded orange jacket,

which brings that color out of the granite of the tower. It is so right, I ask her if she would like me to take her photograph. She smiles and offers me her camera. She is a pleasant young French woman, Emily, who is working in Cordoba. We skirt the lower lake together and ascend along the crest of the huge lateral moraine on the north wall of the valley. Eventually our progress is thwarted by an avalanche chute that knocked the moraine down to a steep scree and talus slope. She wishes she could get out on the ice, but needs to get back to town. I decide to go on. It's a good thing she didn't come because it's hairy—very steep and loose. In the soft slope, every step sends sand, gravel and any hunk of talus nearby tumbling down, and also undermines the same material above, inviting it all to meet my shins. It takes me a long time to descend diagonally about 500 feet to the ice, then I meander among hills of loose gravel floating on the glacier, and eventually arrive at the band of level ice I've been seeking. It allows me to cross the glacier between areas of intense seracs. To the north, the afternoon sun is backlighting the seracs with the tower looming overhead—quite an other-worldly scene. Colors are limited to the whites of ice, the greys of granite, and blues from cyan to cobalt. Crevasses reveal that deep glacial cyan that is found nowhere else but in ancient ice. The same color is deep in the heart of the backlit seracs. These cyans proudly expose themselves, compared to other ethereal, delicate blues that appear in the shadowed ice timidly, as if they are sneaking an opportunity to be seen. The clear sky above the Andes is a dark blue you only see in the mountains and out jetliner windows. Then again, I may have seen the

2008

same color in deep water off the coast of the Caribbean volcanic island of Saint Lucia. The glacier sparkles, a cool wind descends from the spires. Ice crunches underfoot.

Across the glacier I run into an ice-climbing class all decked-out in expedition gear, complete with crampons and hats, gloves, and parkas. I ask if there's a trail on this side of the glacier and am relieved to hear "Si." They're headed that way, but they're slow. As I pass the troop in my t-shirt and hiking boots with my wooden staff, the students, who were previously perfectly happy, are wondering why they are adorned with all the paraphernalia. One asks me if it is difficult without crampons, and I offer a way out for their guides by telling them that I'm used to it because I'm from Alaska, which I suppose is in some way true.

I jam by them, but keep stopping to take photos. My eyes focus on the surface of the ice, two or three steps ahead, then every time I turn around, the sight astounds me again— the view becoming even more spectacular now that I can see farther up the glaciered valley to other smaller but still dramatic towers, called "needles," north of the monarch. In pools of deep clear water penetrating the profound cyan of the inner glacier I see occasional small beds of gravel flung on some sub-surface shelf like a spray of jewels. The wet stones seem polished and on display, their golden and rusty colors contrast-ing with the frosty turquoise. They remind me of sunken trea-sure—precious.

The trail begins right where it makes sense, and it imme-diately climbs six-hundred feet up into the lenga to get around a big cliff. I lose the route where it gets wiped out every winter in an avalanche chute, now housing a cascading stream with loose scree banks, but find my way following paths made by others who have strayed, and reconnect to the main route, which takes me through taller lenga on the way down to the ridgetop of the

2006

southern lateral moraine. From there it's an easy stroll back to the river, and I'm wondering how I'll cross it. I never did learn the answer to that guy's question about the bridge. When I get there I see two ropes spanning the spillway of the river, just below the edge of the lake. There's a zip-line on one, sitting at the far side, but tethered to a retrieving line that is festooned from the rope by a series of carabiners. It's a Tyrollean traverse, probably installed by the guiding companies. I reel it in and, since I don't have a harness, I tie two loops to the zip wheel, using the retrieving line, put my legs through them, and pull myself across.

It's been a long day. Back in camp I cook pasta and pick up the reggae playlist where I left off. U Roy sings "Top of the Peak." It sounds as if I never heard music before, my senses heightened by the day's experience. Music in the back-country is a new luxury for me, and right now it overwhelms me. It's almost too much. It reminds me of driving home from ten-day meditation retreats when I would play one song at a time on the cassette deck in my truck. I couldn't handle the over-stimulus of a second tune without some quiet time to punctuate and separate—to allow a re-settling to the deep peace I had come to dwell in, and a digestion of the music I had just taken in. Now I endure the over-stimulation and feel an overwhelming pleasure from it. My body is giggling when a light blue cabbage butterfly passes by  happily—or, at least it looks happy, the way it flaps its wings and flutters erratically. For all I know it could be having a shitty day, but it makes me feel happy because it is beautiful.

I'm up at 2:15. Two-thirds of a moon is enough to light everything well in the clear air. I go out into the wind, and hike to the lake to look at the mammoth tower. After a few attempts at long exposures I stop and just sit and enjoy. A cold wind is whipping me, and my eyes tear when I look at the tall granite massif glowing in the moonlight like something you'd read about in a Tolkien book. Orion is hanging in the sky over the tower. Down here we see it in the northern sky. I think I see the Southern Cross—my uncertainty due to the fact that I don't know what I'm looking for—right in the Milky Way. Suddenly an image comes to mind—the Australian flag—it reminds me of a fifth star occupying the lower right

quadrant of the cross, and the constellation leaps out of the heavens to my eye. It's not the four stars that make the cross, but the fifth, a red star, that identifies it.

At 5:45 the alarm goes off. In a few seconds I convince myself that it is too early for sunrise, but a few minutes later I notice a golden glow on the tent wall and jump up and rush out to see the first light on the tower. As I climb the terminal moraine that is the dam that creates the lake, the top of the tower already glows a radiant gold, and the line of shadow below it slowly drops as the sun rises. The golden light is astonishing. People who never see these things in nature, but only on film, would expect to hear a symphonic soundtrack to this sunrise, something on the order of Strauss's "Also Sprach Zarathustra."

Naturally I take lots of photos, then retire for a few more hours of sleep. When I rise, others are milling around their tents with cups in hand. I brew some maté for myself, find a boulder to lean back on, and enjoy the bird songs, the way I do on early June mornings on the balcony of my Alaska cabin, listening for the biophany—the local ecosystem's symphony. I listen for the rhythm, the call and response, the layering of high and low notes, and try to open myself to experience a quality I never knew before.

After break-fast and break-camp I visit the lake one last time and pour Aaron Rosewater's water into it. Aaron is a far-out guy I met several years ago who claims to have invented a "machine"—a series of tubes that sends water through several vortexes—that brings water to consciousness. He says his water can bring other water to consciousness simply by contact. So, over the years I've carried small bottles of an ounce or two of his water when I travel, and add the water to special lakes and rivers, glaciers and oceans that I visit. I have no idea about the validity of Aaron's claim, but it's an interesting ritual for me. The point of bringing consciousness to all water is that, since we are over seventy percent water, this could help humanity evolve to a higher consciousness. I know it's a long shot, but what if he is right? As Martin Luther King said, "We will be able to speed up the day, all over America and all over the world, when justice will roll down like waters, and righteousness like a mighty stream."

2008

I head out on the trail and back-track for a few miles to the next terminal moraine—
an older one—where an "unofficial" trail takes off to the north, climbing the spur that sep-
arates two glacial valleys, and crossing that spur at a flat point where two lakes meet end-
to-end and the lenga surrounding them are dwarfed. Progress along the lakeshores slowly

reveals El Chaltén, a 3400-meter tombstone-shaped monolith that
indigenous people dubbed "The Smoking Mountain," also known
as "Monte Fitz Roy." Robert Fitz Roy, Captain of the "Beagle,"
famously giving passage to Charles Darwin, was the first European
to see this granite monument. I'm impressed that he made the long
trip across the pampas, but still I wonder if he deserves having his
name replacing the traditional one, given by the Tehuelche people who lived in these lands
reined by this monarch for 150 centuries. Certainly Fitz Roy deserves such an honor more
than McKinley deserves to displace the Athabaskan name of "Denali," "The Great One,"
and certainly "Fitz Roy" is a more regal name than "McKinley," but I will use "El Chaltén"
in honor of the aboriginal people.

El Chaltén is every bit as impressive as Cerro Torre, so, sensing that the trail is about to
descend into the forest, I lunch in a meadow fifty feet above the trail and watch the mountain.
Below, people hike by without ever seeing me reclining among the hummocks
of grass. I hang out and push my mind towards the insight that I'm looking
for—but all I can come up with is that Nature is divine. My mind can't pene-
trate the unexplored territory without a trail being broken before me. I wonder, "Is the rock *itself* divine, or is it the processes of volcanic intrusion, uplift,
and erosion—the sculptural process, the sculptor—that is divine?" Finally, I

realize that it's a moot point—there's no difference between the two. It's all Nature, and it's
all divine—an expression of ultimate beauty that the human must be intended to observe.

From here, the path drops down, winding its way through woodlands to the camp.
I pass through it and pitch my tent at the upriver end. A rufous-collared sparrow of the
southern race checks me in, and a rusty-tailed woodpecker that I fail to identify also in-
vestigates this newcomer. As soon as my camp is secure, I head out for the high lake called
"Laguna de Los Tres," named by the three French men who first climbed El Chaltén in the
early 50's. Like so many other Argentinean "trails" I've climbed, it's another scramble up a
scree slope, but this time there's a real trail and plenty of exposed bedrock to keep the slope

2008

stable. At the crest I behold the majesty of the monolith. These granite massifs are works of art—sculptures of Nature. To be in their presence is to be in the presence of a master-

piece. Part of the reason that they are masterpieces is because of the natural composition of shapes and sizes. From the perspective of Japanese aesthetics, which I consider to be the most refined aesthetic sense, these rocks are well-arranged. That is, there is a dominant subject—the major peak—accompanied by a subdominant one. Cerro Torre is accompanied by Egger and Standhardt. El Chaltén has the regal tower called "Poincenot" at his side. A third, subordinate, element completes a composition when the beholder moves and the view changes. It could be a glacier below the peaks, or a bonsai lenga in the foreground, a cloud or the moon in the sky, a dark rocky ridge, or a white boulder in a stream at my feet. The subordinate constantly changes. One appreciates these works of aesthetic mastery by viewing them from different angles and in different light, and in different weather, and with different foregrounds.

Most of us observe Nature fairly regularly if not continuously, but the observation is almost always limited because we get conditioned to the experience. In part, we must if we are to get on with the business of survival. It would be overwhelming to live in a forest and be astounded by every tree, every bug, every flower. But in another way we shut ourselves off from the experience of divine Nature by a process the buddhists call "the naming of ten-thousand things." That is, we unconsciously name things "tree," "bug,"

flower," and the naming—the declaration of familiarity—prevents us from seeing the miracle that is right in front of us. When the right mental conditions are present, the sight of a tree, a bug or a flower can jolt us out of our conditioning. Maybe I'm a tough nut to crack. I've usually required big, powerful experiences like an ass-kicking storm, a forest of 360-foot-tall trees, or three weeks floating through the Grand Canyon to knock me out of my conditioned mind and into a state the buddhists call *satori*. But ten-day meditation retreats, and my first intimate tea ceremony, on a quiet winter morning (after a storm when no others were able to attend because of fallen trees blocking roads), have brought me to that state of awareness in which the filters on my perception are diminished. In that state things look more three-dimensional. When I try to explain that, my mind remembers a toy I got for Christmas in about 1960. I was only about three or four years old, but I remember these yellow plastic binocular-looking things. You inserted a cardboard disk with stereoscopic slides into it and looked through

the eye-pieces to see donald duck or mickey mouse leap into the third dimension. For such a youngster the leap from two to three dimensions was almost the same as leaping into reality. Imagine then, the same leap from what we think of as reality to a more vivid world. We are always in that world, but we have conditioned ourselves not to see it. In these last two days glimpses of these towering granite spires woke me up.

It occurs to me that people need to see these colossal carvings—to remind them of the sacredness of Nature, and of the insignificance of "I." If everyone could hike alone here, the world would probably be different. I think better. If they can't come to the mountain, I can bring the mountain to them, through my photographs. I decide to undertake a project: to create a book of photographs of these two sacred, immense sculptures, Cerro Torre and El Chaltén.

The decision feels good. It's an opportunity for me to make a contribution—to help both humanity and the planet. I'm excited.

It's a warm afternoon, and after a few dozen photos I climb out on a rocky point and take a quick dip in the inviting aquamarine tarn at a spot where it is very, very deep. Ice enters the water at the northwest shore where it's fed by a glacier, only a hundred yards away, but the water is surprisingly tolerable. A warm layer, probably in the 50's, must be floating on the surface after a few sunny days.

Before descending, I investigate the outflow of the lake. It falls several hundred feet to the creek that leaves Laguna Sucia, which is in the valley to the south, a few hundred feet below. I'm surprised to see that that lake is green. The name *Sucia* means "dirty," so I was expecting it to be brown or grey, but it's an emerald green, surrounded by granite walls, some below hanging glaciers, some below more granite reaching up to Poincenot. I decide to visit that lake in the morning, and now return to camp to cook dinner while watching the sunset slowly modulate the colors of the thin veil of clouds behind the granite skyscrapers. Again I play with the intense stimulation of music from earbuds. Coltrane's solo in Mile's "Teo" courses down my spine and my head sways to the "Hallelujah!" of his tenor sax. Afterwards I can't take another tune.

In my tent, I set the alarm for five and fall asleep easily even though the Japanese family camped nearby—who have been napping since my return—are up now and talking loudly. But my mind can relax because I don't understand most of it, and before I know it the alarm goes off.

The sky looks good, so I put my wind clothes over the long underwear that I sleep in, add a hat and gloves, and I'm off, using the light of the more-than-half moon overhead. I decide to cross the creek upstream, rather than walk through camp and disturb people, and in doing so I luckily stumble upon a trail that I didn't know about. It's on my side of the creek that drains my destination lake, so I follow it upstream. I enter a stunning forest of bonsai lenga, lit softly by the glow of first light as well as the sunlight reflected off the moon overhead. It's a rare and beautiful light with a hint of rose from the eastern sky that makes it different from the blue moonlight I have skied by in Alaska, and read by in the white sand deserts of the Southwest. Above, the bright stars are still blazing in a navy-blue sky over the towers, which are just becoming illuminated by the rosy glow.

The forest peters out, overtaken by the white granite boulders of the glacial outwash plain. This is that kind of granite that has no distinct cleavage. Rather than fracture easily, it breaks like Styrofoam, and for that reason is very resistant. I once saw men try to blast this kind of rock in Prince William Sound. They had a hard time and ended up overloading the drill holes with explosives to get the stuff to break. They sent one very large doniker a few hundred feet up and out into the bay towards a landing craft that was at anchor. The rumor was that the skipper of the landing craft shit his pants when he saw that massive rock descending towards him, but it landed beside the boat.

The valley bends and gets tighter, and an outcrop pinches the side I'm on so I have to do a little climbing traverse to get around it without getting wet. But still I'm at the lake well before sunrise, so I sit back in the hollow of a comfortable boulder the size of a small truck, and wait. A flock of birds flies by and stops to visit. They act like snow buntings, but wear a black mask, and are light-bellied and covered with dappled grey and black stripes. I can't find them in my book.

A mackerel sky moves in, and after it receives a deep dark pink from the sun on the horizon, the eastern edge of each puff is illuminated in a color that reminds me of the fuchsias in Chile, the color lightens and hits the top of El Chaltén, the main tower, and works its way down, shifting to a brilliant gold. When the sun enters a strata of thin clouds in the

east, the light flattens. The whole event lasts about fifteen minutes. But then sunlight occasionally finds a line-of-sight through the clouds and strikes the granite in patches for moments, punctuating long lulls of aluminum light. I sit and watch, listening to the thunder of huge chunks of ice falling somewhere above. I hear this five or six times, always searching for the source, never seeing any movement at all on the glaciers.

As I descend the valley towards camp, the sun frees itself from the clouds and relights the peaks. A young guy with long blonde hair backpacks by while I'm on top of a house-sized rock in the middle of the creek taking photographs. When I hit the bonsai forest I wander around in it, stopping to admire many of the plant sculptures, and trying to frame a photo, which is not easy.

Breakfast eaten and camp struck, I follow the trail heading north along the Rio Blanco, which drains the entire area. In a few miles the trail crosses the creek draining Laguna Piedras Blancas, to the west. I stash my pack in a cranny and follow the creek up through granite rocks the size of cars and garages to the small lake in a freshly-gorged valley which looks like it must have been full of ice less than a thousand years ago. Laguna Piedras Blancas is not white, but a milky jade. A menacing glacier hangs above it, intensely seraced, and flowing down from the north side of El Chaltén, which is only partly visible, partly hidden by a ridge in the foreground.

Back on the trail, I run into an Aussie who was on my bus from El Calafate. We trade stories of our hikes. My route crosses a barbed-wire fence on a boulder pile where the trail leaves the park. I'm looking for a fork so I can take a short-cut to the north/northwest. The river I've been following bends to the east, but I continue following a dwindling trail (it is "unofficial" I'm rationalizing), which eventually disappears. I'm leaving the wide, flat gravel-and-sand outwash plain of the Rio Blanco, and crossing a sand flat with just enough scrub to keep you from seeing too far when I realize I missed my turn, but don't want to turn back to find it. The trail I missed would cut the acute angle between Rio Blanco and the river to its north, which flows east to their confluence. If I just head north, I will eventually cross the trail heading up that river, Rio Electrico. I check my map to be sure I have the right idea, and trudge on in the sugary sand, which yields to my weight and the forward push of my toes. It's mid-afternoon and hot. I run out of water. I'm hungry, but

I want to hit the trail, and the river, and shade before stopping. I push on with Eddie Grant's "Electric Avenue" in my head, wondering why they named the river "Electric." Finally I find a horse trail and it's heading to the north-northwest—just right—but it slowly begins bending to the north, then north-northeast, and then northeast. I grumble while waiting for it to swing back to the west, but finally have to admit I'm going the wrong way. So I turn around and head back. After passing the place where I found it,  the trail heads off to the southwest, leaving the river. I follow it grumbling more, and eventually abandon it because I don't like the southerly trend. Once again, I take off through the scrubby forest, heading north for the river. In a few hundred yards I see another horse trail. I don't remember ever having hit a trail and turning the wrong way in my life, but here I do it twice in a row, which tells me I'm more tired than I want to admit. After a few hundred more yards I hit the river and the trail bends to the east, so I curse and stop for lunch, soaking my burning feet in the icy river.

I'm hungry, so after a couple sandwiches I keep reaching for more dried apricots. Then I do the only thing I can do, and turn around to follow this trail wherever it goes. It takes me to the southwest and I mumble protests, but stay with it, thinking it might be circling a swamp. Eventually it rises to the toe of the mountain, entering the forest, and merges with the real trail, which is still an "unofficial" one. At the junction my trail is blocked off with several dead branches, indicating that it's the wrong way to go.

Now I'm happier, but the sugar in my dessert of *demascas desecadas* stimulated my pancreas to produce insulin and remove the excess sugar from my blood. The problem now is that it seems to have removed *all* the sugar from my blood, and I bonk. In hospitable

grassy woodland, where the trees are tall and a cool breeze is blowing off the river below, I shed pack and boots, and lounge.

A day-hiker comes along; a Kiwi, older than me. We have a pleasant conversation. He must be a doctor because when I tell him I bonked, he tells me I'll be fine in fifteen minutes when my blood sugar returns. He's right. After he leaves I get on the trail and feel fine. An easy forty-five-minute walk through the cool green woods brings me to a refugio called "Fraile" where they charge fourteen pesos to camp in a fenced yard in the lee of a roche moutonnée. The guidebook says it's a huge erratic, but I disagree. The gentle slope

facing the retreated glacier and the jagged vertical wall that protects this camp from the glacial wind are typical of a glacial-worn outcrop of resistant bedrock. The glacier wore the upstream side down to a ramp. Water penetrated the cracks in the rock and refroze. As the ice left the trailing edge of the outcrop, it plucked chunks of rock off, leaving this blocky wall that looks like some giant stole the other half of the hill. It is a classic roche mouton-  née. The cool grass feels delightful on my bare feet. I was hoping to climb the pass above this place to get a view of the towers from this angle, but my afternoon took more out of me than expected, so I decide to rest and make the climb at 4:30 in the morning. I begin meal preparations in a cook shelter and fall into conversation with the blond-haired kid I saw early in the morn- ing. He didn't miss the trail junction and beat me here. He tells me he's from Chile, but I understand his Spanish well, and that confuses me because I have such a hard time with Chilean "Castillano." He wants to climb the pass in the morning too.

My bag calls me early, and I set the alarm for four. At 3:58 I wake to the sound of rain, so I return to sleep, waking again three hours later, feeling rested. It's still raining, so I make tea in the shack. After breakfast the Chilean kid comes in, bedraggled. He didn't let the rain stop him, and he climbed toward the pass at dawn. He said it was so windy that there were times when he had to crawl, but he did get a glimpse of El Chaltén during a brief break in the storm and saw it behind a rainbow. Fortune favors the brave.

It turns out that the reason I understand his Spanish so well is that he is a German who just moved to Chile a year ago to teach outdoor education to kids.

 Leaving the compound, I pause at the gate to admire the peaks above when a break in the fast-moving clouds reveals them for a minute. The Danish woman who was camped near me walks up to the gate, so we naturally become hiking partners. She's a social worker in the Denmark winter, a hiking guide in the Greenland summer, and has recently begun to train in aikido because of trouble with drunken clients. She is just arriving to the area, coming down a small road from Chile, where she reports that the traveling was good but slow, hopping from town to town on the sin- gle bus that typically runs every other day. I'm back-tracking along Rio Electrico, but after I pass the familiar closed trail junction, I'm on the route I missed yesterday, which leads me

2008

back to a large cairn on the Rio Blanco gravel that indicates the trail junction. I walked right by it yesterday.

I find it entertaining that we never know each other's names. I let it go intentionally, and when we hit the creek to Laguna Piedras Blancas I tell her it is worth seeing, and that I'm going to climb the lateral moraine for a view. She opts for the easy route, taking the creek bed, and we never see each other again.

It took some time to scale the loose scree and talus slope above the creek, but at the top I cross the edge of a forest mat. The climb up the ridge of the moraine in the young forest is steep, but the views are rewarding.

I have lunch on a promontory, a zigzag of the break, facing up-valley with my lower legs hanging off the edge of the forest into the air among roots above the plummeting scree. I see the spec of the Dane wander-ing through the boulders below, and realize she cannot see me even if she was looking right at me. My khaki-colored pants and green rain-jacket are the perfect camouflage for my situation. Maybe this is part of the reason that a flock of parakeets flies right at me before they see me and chatter up into the wind above the vast void between the walls of the parallel moraines.

This little valley has two huge lateral moraines pushing into the large river valley below at ninety degrees. Both are forested on their back-sides, and completely barren on the inside, where constant decay of the loose scree prevents any vegetation from taking hold. It's not been too long since this gravel was deposited. I imagine it happening—the power of a glacier eating up a mountain and spitting it out. Witnessing the aftermath of such intense glaciation leads me to wonder what it must be like to live in an era of glacial advance, when walls of ice would bulldoze mature forests. The image of old-growth timber being slowly swallowed by an advancing glacier is one I never created before.

Due to global climate change, the vast majority of the Earth's glaciers are retreating. A recent study revealed that over ninety-eight percent of Alaska's glaciers are. So much ice is leaving the mountains that both NASA and the USGS predict that "The Great Land" will

2008

be having more earthquakes as the earth's crust rebounds after the released load, and that these quakes will cause more tsunamis.

As the glaciers melt, water collects under them and lubricates them so they travel more quickly, resulting in an even greater rate of melting. When ice melts, revealing rock or dirt, the albedo, or reflectivity, of that area drops dramatically. Ice has a very high reflectivity; rock and soil's reflectivity is much lower, depending on its darkness. The more land that is revealed in a valley, the more heat it will absorb from the sun, warming the valley even more, and melting more ice. The same thing happens in the oceans. The enormous influx of fresh water into the polar seas has changed the salinity so much that it has already slowed the Earth's ocean thermo-haline conveyor current by thirty percent. This current is driven by once-warm waters that sink after reaching high latitudes in the North Atlantic where they become densely saline, after excessive evaporation, and sink. The introduction of fresh water from melting ice on land and sea lessens the density of the water, weakening the "pump." Without this thermo-haline conveyor the higher latitudes will cool and the lower latitudes, unable to lose heat via the current, will warm. Glaciers may then begin to grow again, not only in Alaska, but especially in Europe, which is ice-free now only because of warm waters reaching it from the tropical Atlantic, the Gulf of Mexico, and the Caribbean. The big problem is that once the conveyor stops, it takes hundreds of years to get going again.

A condor soars high overhead. Fields of sunlight traverse the slopes of rock and ice as the storm breaks. I climb the ridge towards the ice, crossing a sweet, flat, sandy depression, possibly formed when a buried chunk of ice melted. It would be a fine camp if one were willing to carry water up here. Above, El Chaltén is living up to its name ("The Smoking Mountain") with a plume of white seeming to be anchored to its peak, but actually, it's constantly being generated at the peak and dissipating at the trailing edge.

I descend, retrieve my pack from the cave where I stashed it, and eat up the trail, my pack minus the weight of a pasta dinner, a little dry milk and cereal, two tea bags, some salami, cheese and bread. I jam back to the double-log bridge crossing the river where a young Israeli stops me, asking for directions. I'm trying to give him the complete lay of the land, but he keeps interrupting me to tell me what he wants to know. I

2008

interrupt his interruption and tell him to listen, finish telling him where everything is, and continue down.

While descending, the scene behind me grows more dynamic as the storm clouds seem to be torn apart by a wild, gusty gale, and sunlight splashes the spires, so I clamber through brush off the trail to get some shots. In doing so I discover a pretty little beach below a tiny falls that charms me—a good place to bivouac if one were to climb up here after leaving town late in the day. This spot might offer exquisite photos in the morning sun, but I still try to get some now.

My descent continues through forest, eventually breaking out to the canyon of the big river flowing from the north, the Rio de las Vueltas, which now contains all the water I have seen in the past few days. It looks like a canyon in Eastern Washington or British Columbia. Another classic roche moutonnée hunkers in the valley floor, confirming that my suspicion about the rock upwind from last night's camp is more than justified. I wander out on a promontory, come across some calafate bushes loaded with berries, and enjoy a small feast. They're very similar to blueberries.

Three Sunrises

Soon I'm in town, making camp and getting a shower at El Refugio. I drop in at La Casita for a repeat of the steak dinner I had the night before I left on the trail. I improve it by having a carafe instead of a glass of cabernet. The carafe is a ceramic white penguin. The pony-tailed waiter further improves my dinner by adding a fine salad with shredded carrots and beets on the usual lettuce and tomato. Vegetables are rare in the restaurants of Chile and Argentina. These are the first I've had in a month. It's crowded, so after dinner I surrender my table to a couple, and retire with the last of my vino to a small table in the back corner where they park their chocolate cake. The smell is too much for me, my resistance

being lowered by the wine, and I enjoy a slice on the house, which is excellent with the fruity cabernet that carries a hint of cherry. By the time I'm finished I'm thinking of a cigar, but the Dominican that I've been hauling around is in my tent. So I drop in at the bar next door for a nightcap.

The bartender, Cristian, is quite friendly and after some conversation he asks me to translate his menu. I tell him that that sounds like work, so he fills my scotch whiskey glass. I accept the job, but accepting the pay is a bad idea.

I tell him if he wants to appeal to North Americans and Europeans, he should offer vegetables. He asks me what I mean. I tell him that we're used to eating vegetables, they're important for health, but they're never in restaurants in the southern cone. "What kind of vegetables?" he asks. Rather that go into a long list of produce, I tell him that I was at the market earlier and saw green beans there. Why not offer steamed green beans? They're excellent with a little butter and salt. He makes a note of it, and I get to work on the menu. Some of my translations are not literal so I explain them, like "Hamburguesa Completa," becoming, "Hamburger with the works."

An Irishman enters. He's in his fifties, owns a steel fabrication plant in his home country, and loves to travel and meet people. His name is Tom too, and he takes a liking to me, buys me a drink, explains his motto, his three D's: "Decide, Delegate, Disappear" and looks at me with a satisfaction, as if I now have the key to life. After eyeing the menu he asks me if I know where he can get some vegetables. I call Cristian over and tell him what the Irishman is asking for. The point is well-taken.

Cristian kept filling my glass. Like I said, it was a bad idea to accept the pay. I ended up moving slow in the morning with a *caña*. I guess they use the word because it's

like getting hit in the head with a cane. It's a late start, crossing town to the south end, near the park headquarters, where I take the trail that heads out towards the Viedma Glacier to the southwest. Another trail branches off of it and heads up to tree line, below a sombrero-shaped peak called "Pliege Tumbado," literally something like "knocked-down fold." My plan is to take this route and make camp below tree line, then climb the peak, but the whole point of the venture is to catch the first light of day tomorrow. A team of pack-horses takes the trail

2008

ahead of me. I stay within sight of them 'til the first climb, when the horses open the distance. The trail passes through fields grazed by livestock. I'm reminded of a climb I did in Ansel Adams Wilderness of the Sierra Nevada, when I was disappointed to see cow pies all over the grassy back-side of the peak. A few years later, when I was backpacking in the Owyhee canyons of Southeast Oregon, I realized the degree of devastation inflicted by cattle when I stomped past cattle tracks and manure in sparsely vegetated canyon floors until I hit a natural rock pile blockading the canyon. Beyond the rocks, where the cattle couldn't go, it was another world, filled with tall ferns, rushes, horsetails, and an abundance of herbs. When I returned home I wanted to write a letter to the Bureau of Land Management to complain about the cattle, so I educated myself on the law. On the long list of designated uses for wilderness areas, all are recreational but one: grazing. The cow pies in Ansel Adams wilderness were legal, but the destruction in the remote reaches of the Owyhee canyon network was not, because the river is designated as Wild and Scenic, and grazing is forbidden.

It's an easy climb through the forest. The trail follows a stream for a long time, then leaves it, and the lenga soon shrink. When I see them begin to spread over the ground, I stop and descend for a minute before heading off the trail to find a tent site. It's not legal to camp here, so I hide behind a thicket. After camp is set, I descend to the stream and fill pots and bottles with water, stash them at camp, put a bottle in my lumbar pack and take off for the peak.

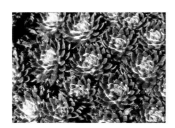

Leaving tree line is like walking out of a house—it's that drastic a break. Tundra takes over for a mile, yields to rock, and from there up it's a moonscape. A bench on the northern flank attracts me, and I detour by it and get some great views. The reason to ascend Pliege Tumbado is that it has views of both Cerro Torre and El Chaltén, and I'm taking them both in with pleasure. It's my first opportunity to do so. A climber I met told me he thought of El Chaltén as the masculine and Cerro Torre as the feminine of a royal pair—the king and queen. "Fitz," he explained, "has broad shoulders and is huge. Torre is slender, graceful and has that hint of an hour-glass shape." It makes perfect sense to me as they both stand before me like enormous chess pieces.

Continuing on, I make the peak sooner than expected. A rare event. Usually a climber is fooled by a false summit which, when crested, reveals more climbing. Sometimes this

happens more than once. The view from the peak is good, but it's a mountain-top view—there are limited possibilities for creating a composition. The view *is* the composition. Besides, the late afternoon light does not flatter these east-facing peaks, so, unless the clouds are performing well, there is no art to be made. I lounge on the peak with anorak hood cinched tightly around my face to help me endure the wind, and watch the light change as the sun sinks toward the Pacific. When it drops behind the mountains, I drop to camp, making dinner as the sky darkens and the stars brighten, set my alarm for five, and crash. Last night's scotch has me tired, and, as they say in Japan, "Shin da yo ni nemaru," I sleep like a dead man.

It's a cold morning with stars twinkling in a black sky. My water bottle has a little ice in it. I deny myself the luxury of savoring another moment of the warmth of my bag, and force myself into clothes and boots, take a slug of ice water, leave my headlight on, and head for the high country. By the time I leave the tundra the eastern sky is rosy. Mud at a stream crossing is frozen yet plastic under foot. I reach the bench before the sun reveals itself and set up for the show. When the first rays ignite the peaks, it's not as dramatic as the last two times I saw this because of the greater distance, but nevertheless I'm pleased. Afterwards, I traverse the north slope, westward from the bench for about a kilometer, until I get the composition I want, with a dark jagged ridge—a buttress of Cerro Solo—creating a complementary foreground to the dominant lines of Cerro Torre. Fox tracks cross the sandy scree. On the way down I play with photographing tiny tundra flowers.

After I reach the bottom, while crossing town, a guy with glasses and a red crew-cut encounters me as he exits the grocery store. He asks where I've been, and we walk together on the long north-south artery of the frontier hamlet. He says his name is Antonio. He's from Poland. I guess he changed his name to suit the language here—a trend I could never understand. Personal names don't change when you cross international boundaries. Few Hispanics change from Juan to John when coming north, but most Johns change to Juan when going south. It makes no sense. Antonio is a climber and adventurer. He's waiting for a stretch of good weather to go up Rio Electrico, past its source at the terminus of the Marconi Glacier, and up the glacier to the pass with the same name, where it joins the Great Southern Icefield. He tells me it's the third-largest icefield in the world after Antarctica and Greenland. He's interested in crossing the length of it, from north to south—a trip of a couple-hundred miles. Right now he just wants to go see it, and spend a night in a tiny

2008

shelter some mountaineers built at the foot of a nearby mountain, across the Chilean border. He invites me to join him, and I take him up on the offer, as the pass will offer views of the granite towers from the northwest. But he wants to wait a few days for the coming storm to pass, so we agree to leave in three or four days. He encourages me to camp at the free campsite where I spent my first night, tells me that the back end is full of climbers, guides, and porters working for guiding companies, that everyone watches out for each other there, and I can get a shower for four pesos at the big hostel nearby. I feel obligated to spend another night at El Refugio, since they are guarding my gear. But I'll come visit him in the morning. I make camp behind the old hippie's place, get a shower and try a new restaurant. El Muro, "The Wall," is a very hip place—beat, I would say—and maybe that's because it's run by an aging woman of that generation. The food is excellent; a fat grass-fed steak with potatoes and onions all roasted on the same fire. I'm "belly-full and body-glad," as a Belizean diver taught me to say, and head back to my tent for the night.

In the morning I visit the free camp, "Madsen." I ask climbers for Antonio and they direct me to the tent of *El Polaco Loco*. He's not there, but a neighbor is. She is Evelyn, a sweet Argentinean with long brown hair and big green eyes. She offers me maté, so we sit and chat while passing the gourd. We become friends quickly. She's here to work as a porter, carrying supplies in her backpack to remote camps hosting tourists, spending the summer doing what she loves, walking in the mountains. She suggests that I camp beside her and use her kitchen tent to store my gear.

I take her up on the storage offer, but decide to take advantage of the predicted day-and-a-half before the next storm to go up for more photos of The Smoking Mountain.

During the ascent I feel strong. Maybe it's the maté, maybe I'm getting in shape. Probably it's both. At the high camp, just as I move into my tent, a crew of four shows up and camps nearby. One of them is a woman from The States. Not only is her voice the loudest in camp, but I can understand the words without trying, so I plug into the iPod, hit my "Afrojazz" playlist, and cook pasta in minestrone soup while anticipating the sunset. My camera is strapped to a dead lenga branch overhead while I sit and eat with eyes on the peaks. Just as the colors begin, a bank of clouds moves in from the west and smothers the heads of the giants. I just hope the morning is different, and absorb Archie Shepp's version of "No Agreement."

When the alarm goes off I feel rested, and when I see stars above, I head out for my chosen destination, Cerro Madsen. Like the free camp north of town, it's named for Andreas Madsen, the first *probador*, or settler, in this area. Once I'm out of the trees I see headlights on the switchbacks. Three or four others have the same idea—to be at Laguna de los Tres before sunrise—but they're a half-hour ahead of me, causing me to doubt my timing. So I shift into high gear. By the time I'm half-way up the switchbacks I'm in a t-shirt even though the temperature is in the 30's. At the top I beeline for Madsen, across the top of the terminal moraine that holds the Laguna. My timing is perfect. I'm on the south flank of Madsen when the light begins. I couldn't have gone any further without the buttress of Madsen obscuring El Chaltén. My microfleece top and anorak come out

of my pack, and the show begins. You can never predict what will happen from the interplay between the distant clouds in the east, which block the sunlight, and the local clouds

constantly forming and dissipating around the peaks, often times hiding them. It's a good show even though The Smoking Mountain is living up to its name and maintaining a cloud like a turban around its head. The grand finale surprises me when a horizontal band of copper light sweeps down the massif to its bottom. Just as I think it's gone, it hits the very ground I'm standing on and illuminates the talus I occupy with that rich red-gold light while the high rock is shaded.

Certain that I got some good photos, my excitement takes me up Madsen like a machine even though I question the safety of the climb on loose rock and hard, steep snow as much as I do the necessity of this vertical campaign. I remember a long time ago when I ate

psilocybin mushrooms and began a long hike to a chosen destination. I don't think I got a half-mile before I realized how ridiculous it was to insist on reaching the destination. It was clear that the journey was what was to be enjoyed. I spent the day wandering inside of a half-acre of forest, and had plenty to see. Of course, that was in an old-growth forest of giant redwoods, but ever since then it has been easier for me to let go of goals if it seems the wise thing to do. This morning I never even consider it. I'm too thrilled with the beauty and the anticipation of my photographs and the book I will make. I really feel as if I'm in a groove—like I am doing the best thing I can possibly be doing at this time in my life, and that things are falling into place because of it.

The final eighty feet to the peak requires both hands, so I stash my staff and go up. The hand-holds are good and the climb is easy. The pinnacle is made of two vertical slabs—two halves of the same rock—with one having slid down fifteen feet. The top of the lower one is ninety degrees to the plane of sheer, and both are tilted away from Fitz at about fifteen degrees. The result of this arrangement is a comfortable bench facing the giant. The only drawback is the large deposit of condor guano on half of the bench. I'm sitting at 1806 meters, 1056 meters above camp.

The monarch is playing peek-a-boo in the clouds. I have no reason to descend other than intensifying hunger, and I'm thrilled to be in the presence of the divine, so I hang out for a couple hours and watch him come and go, and the occasional splash of sunlight that slips be-tween the clouds behind me. All the while I lis-ten to the thunder of calving ice and avalanches. Usually the source of these roars is impossible to find in the vast ex-panse of ice before me, but to-day my eye finds a few chunks of ice flying before a black rock wall. With no small amount of luck, a hanging glacier in the same neighborhood re-leases the volume of a large office building, and I watch it fall to the glacier below and explode in silence. Blocks the size of cars and trucks tumble down the surface of the iceflow, and as they

slow, the crack and thunderous rumble finally reaches my ear. The sudden realization comes

that, until now, I could never find the source of the thunder because it's always over by the time I hear it. This cataclysm was relatively near. Those in the distance have come to rest before the reverberations between the mountain walls reach me. Some black blocks of rock slide slowly down the white slope and disappear in crevasses the way black grains of sand get caught in the cracks of a bar of soap left in an outdoor shower for a few years.

A bank of clouds rises from the west and engulfs the tall granite. At the same time a bitter, damp wind hits my peak. I take it as a cue to descend to my staff and search for an alternate route down that is safer than my ascent. Cerro Madsen is a peak on a ridge radiating from the base of El Chaltén. After the cerro, this ridge splits and descends to the valley of Rio Blanco. Retracing my steps down the south buttress seems a bit dicey, so I explore the northern one, but I can't see past a series of pinnacles right below me. Every time I reach a col, I see more loose, steep talus to traverse, more steep, spiky obstacles to skirt, and all this with an incomplete view. The further I go the less I'll want to abandon this route, which means the more chances I will take to get down this way, so I begin cursing every time I decide to go down without knowing what lies ahead. The route is precarious—steep, loose, slippery and sharp—and demands concentration. I keep telling myself, "I don't fall" (occasionally out loud) and eventually I sneak out of the situation and gain the spine of the ridge, less steep and more

solid, where I notice the view again now that the stress is gone. Those end-to-end lakes I took so long to pass a few days ago look like a bootprint from here. Laguna Madre is the sole, Laguna Hija is the heel. Beyond them is Laguna Capri, then a vast ocean of pampas stretching to the Atlantic, too far away to see.

Further down I decide to cross the snowfield between the two buttresses. It's steep, but it faces east, so the filtered sun has already corned the top few inches. Using my staff as an ice axe, I can arrest a slip and fall before I go into an accelerating slide down to the sharp talus at the top of a couloir far below. Once I'm three-quarters the way across, the fall below me is only eighty yards and ends in glacier-polished outcroppings that don't look so menacing, so I allow myself to glissade to them. They're the color of steel plate that has sat in raging water for years—rusted, yet polished. I'm reminded of fallen trains in whitewater rivers, or shipwrecks on the beaches of the Pacific Northwest.

2008

By the time I reach Laguna de los Tres I'm feeling the effects of a fuel gauge on 'E,' but I cross the spillway where the water tumbles down to Laguna Sucia, and explore the

high route over the cliffs on the south side of the lake. This is the climbers' access to the base of El Chaltén. I heard it was hairy, so I wanted to check it out. It's nothing compared to what I just did, but it would be more challenging with a full pack. I like the idea of taking this route and climbing the glacier to "Paso Superior," where I could sleep in snow caves and catch dawn's first light on the massif from its very base. But that's another trip—one that I'd like to be roped to a couple of partners for.

While descending I'm trying to take my mind where it's never been... and feeling stuck. I'm wrestling with the concept of earth processes—those responsible for these sculptures—being divine, intelligent, and whether the processes are separable from the matter they work on. I can't find a differ-

ence. Wind, rain, ice—it's all matter. Vulcanism, evaporation, expansion and contraction, freezing—it's all chemistry and physics. It's the interaction of matter. I look down at the talus I'm crossing and it's clearly of the same stuff, and probably broke off of El Chaltén. So if El Chaltén is divine, why wouldn't this rock I'm stepping on now be? If this rock is, why not that one over there? The whole scree slope. Why not the whole damn planet? What did Jesus say? "The kingdom of God is at hand."

My legs and feet are tired when I make it to camp at 3:30. I devour two olive loaf and cheese sandwiches while boiling water for instant mashed potatoes. The five servings of spuds take a while to finish, then I take a nap.

The sunset hour draws me out of the tent, but dark clouds block any hope for color. On the way back from the outhouse I see a tired man sitting on a log who looks like he could use some cheer. He's got a red hat and red parka on, with a compass hanging from his neck by a red cord. My guess is that he's a North American, so I initiate conversation in English, "Hard day?" Roger is a sixty-five-year-old physical therapist from Medford, Oregon. He loves to travel, and says he figured he better come hike Patagonia while his knees can still take it. They're sore now. He just came up from Lago Torre today, and climbed from this camp to Laguna de los Tres—it's the same trip I did on my second day here. We talk about good hikes in the area. He consults his compass to verify the direction when he points to a place that he knows from the map. When I ask, he tells me he's carried a com-

pass when traveling for years—he can't stand getting turned around, losing his orientation and not knowing which way is north. He broke his foot thirty years ago and it's beginning to bother him on days like this. I've got a dozen injuries that could come back to haunt me as I age. I imagine myself in his situation in only fifteen years. I see myself sitting on that log—white hair, sore knees, refusing to give up. His backpacking days are numbered, but as a whitewater rafter, he will be able to get his wilderness time on river trips for many more years. While we're talking I see a fresh hawk feather on the ground and offer it to him, but he declines, so I stick it in my hat. We trade cards and agree to be in touch for whitewater trips in Oregon.

In the morning the remnants of howling wind and rain on the peaks are tossed at my tent. When the sunrise alarm goes off, I go out to pee. There's no color on the obscured granite. A fine rain falls. All the tents are closed and silent. Two carranchos walk through camp, silently searching for scraps. Now I know where the hawk feather came from. A flock of parakeets darts by while I'm making maté from my tent door.

Soon I'm on the trail. At a swamp crossing, a tiny frog lies in the path, incapacitated

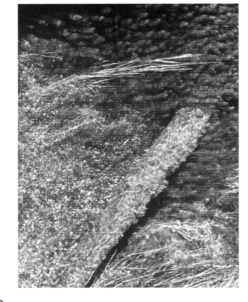

by the cold. It's a bright green with brilliant yellow lon-gitudinal stripes. Maybe my fingers warmed it when I moved it to the grass. It's one thing that the many predators here can eat. Yesterday I saw some lizards. There's supposed to be a kind of desert rat here, but the campers in Madsen leave their food in old worn-out tents with zippers bro-ken by gusts of the pervasive high winds, and no one ever has a mouse problem, so there can't be too many of them. There seem to be lots of predators but no prey. What do the puma eat? Foxes? What do the foxes eat? Only the introduced rabbit is abundant enough to support these predators, and I suppose the condors clean up after every meal. Strange though, how those giant scavengers prefer to ride the high mountain winds, far from the rabbits in the lowlands.

In town I make camp in Madsen, and Evelyn invites me to join her and her friends for dinner. Of course I accept, but I know they eat late so I check to be sure, then go out to El Muro for another fine meal in the late afternoon when most restaurants are closed. I'll

eat again with them later, in typical Argentina style. I'm happy to be invited by this tall, attractive young woman, but the strange thing is that I feel no sexual energy coming from her at all. It is as if she's in a balloon that insulates her from that energy coming from me. It's fascinating.

At ten, Evelyn and I cross town on foot, in strong gusts carrying sheets of spray, to the internet lounge. Once we began walking together her gait explains her nonsexual vibe. She's tight in the hips and legs, with an overemphasized use of the quadriceps and tibialis muscles to initiate the leg's forward swing. Her stride faintly resembles that of the Tin Man. What I sense is that the musculature of her legs is still expressing shock, after many years. This sense is one that I developed from intense training and then working with hundreds of people as a somatic therapist. It's sad to think that she was molested or maybe raped when she was younger. No wonder she told me that she'd never get married. No wonder she feels so good when she hikes and uses the muscles that wanted to carry her away in flight from her abuser.

We arrive at 10:30, and I meet her friends, Fernando, the owner of the business, and his Australian girlfriend, Tarina. We begin cooking around eleven, and eat pasta in a marinara sauce some time around midnight. In conversation I mention that the wind wears on me. Fernando starts telling stories about the wind. He says that last winter it blew two of his car windows out. And 250 kilometer-per-hour gusts picked up the log benches outside his shop and threw them a block downwind. It's hard for me to imagine.

After dinner we watched a movie. By the time I got in my sleeping bag it was almost three, and I had been up since my pre-dawn alarm, so I slept and dozed under rain on the tent as long as I could, then spent the day hanging out with Evelyn and her friend Waldo, a climber from the north of the country who is escaping the intense heat of his desert mountain home, working as a porter here in cool Patagonia. Waldo is an angular man, with broad level shoulders above a wide but trim waist. His face is well-chisled, with a triangular nose, and his hair, parted well to the side, is combed across the top of his head, making it flat. I get to like Waldo more each time I interact with him. I call him "Señior Tranquilo" because he's one of the calmest, most laid-back and soft-spoken men I've met among adventurers. He plans to climb El Chaltén with his buddy, Indio.

Rain sounds like static on the tent roof, over our conversation which continues for hours. I can't find Antonio. He's not in his tent all day.

2008

After a couple days of hanging with the Argentineans waiting for the storm to pass, the stars come out and I still can't find El Polaco Loco. So, in the morning I make a new plan—to hike back up Rio Electrico and try again for Paso Cuadrado. I assume I can hitchhike to the trailhead, and I would have been correct if I had left at a reasonable hour, but it's almost noon by the time I get on the road, and I eventually realize that there will be no traffic at all. It's an eighteen-kilometer walk on the unscreened glacial till roadbed in an intense headwind that I lean into. The storm has passed, but around here an intense wind continues to howl for a day after the rain, as if it's chasing the clouds away. I'm tired before I find the trailhead. Luckily, it's an easy hike up the river to the trail that I know. I'm in the same parkland neighborhood of mature lenga that I was in when I had the blood-sugar crash from the dried apricots, this time traveling quickly on the easy trail, when I crest a small hill and see a full-grown puma about fifty yards ahead.

I've heard them a few times—once in the Anza-Borrego desert while reading by the light of a midnight moon in a remote camp. In an effort to verbally articulate the sound when I returned from the trip, I concluded that it sounded like a twelve-year-old-boy imitating a woman screaming in horror. Years later I was sitting naked on a sauna step, steaming in the cool night air of the Sierra foothills when I heard it again. "What was that?" My friend thought it must be the new neighbors on her unpopulated dirt road. My mind took about fifteen seconds to remember where I had heard it before, and she validated that a lion had been spotted in the area that week.

I saw the ass-end of one as it ran into the bushes while I was driving into the Lost Coast of Northern California, but this is the first time I've stood facing a big cat. "Holy shit!" involuntarily leaves my mouth as I freeze and it slinks off for cover. It's big—about five feet from nose to butt, with a long tail drooping down to the ground then curving back. I'm stunned to see that it's the homogenous velvety grey-brown of a Weimariner, with no distinct markings anywhere but on its face—unusual for a wild animal. Its head and torso are slung low from the two scapula protruding from its back as it trots in that cat way that allows horizontal movement without vertical movement—a way that is imitated by Japanese martial artists.

The headwind hid my scent and sound, the hill hid my sight, and I surprised the cat. It almost seemed embarrassed that I caught it in the open, and in a few seconds it's in the cover of the brush near the river.

Standing still for a few minutes, I take in the experience. If it were a bear, I'd be fairly sure that it was gone, but cats are sneaky. So when I begin hiking again I keep an eye

towards the brush where it took cover. Once past it, I have to keep turning around a couple times a minute to be sure it's not stalking me. It seems likely that it watched me as I passed. The ground in this park-woods is grassy, but littered with the dead bodies of trees taken down by the williwaws that have ripped down this valley for centuries. Because I'm traveling upriver, the logs lay roughly parallel to the trail, and their grey-brown color is the perfect cover for the furtive feline. I've watched enough house-cats stalk birds and rodents to imagine how the puma would advance behind the logs. I stop and look for a pair of yellow-green eyes burning in the shadows below logs that curve into the air. If I find them, I can intimidate the cat by staring at it—something I would never try with a grizzly. I keep my senses dialed to full power, with my mouth open. I don't know why I do that when I want to hear well. Maybe it lets out the sound of blood racing through my carotid arteries. Even when I decide that it's long gone, like a turkey through the corn, I don't trust it enough to turn my back on it, and I keep turning back on occasion to be sure. I know it would be intimidated by my size with this backpack on, but can it sense my fatigue? I shift my attitude to one of strength and confidence, like I own these woods, and proceed with more and more comfort.

The funny thing is that just a few minutes before this encounter I was thinking about the lion butt I saw on the Lost Coast. I was thinking about a conversation I had the day before with Evelyn about pumas. She has only seen the same—the butt end of one as it ran into bushes for cover. This reminds me of the movie we watched last night at Fernando's, "What the #%* Do We Know?" Part of the film's message is that we have the power to create reality with our minds. Is it a coincidence that I saw a puma just after I was thinking of one? I think so. Once I stood on the bow of an Alaskan ferry telling a friend a story about dolphins playing in the bow-wave of some boat I worked on, and within a minute a pod of Dall's porpoises were below us acting as if they heard everything I said—probably coincidence again, but we had a good laugh because it seemed like I summoned them. Countless times I have told stories of animals or thought of them without them making an

2008

appearance, and often thankfully so, since a few times white shark stories were related to other surfers as we sat like bait bobbing beyond the breakers.

It occurs to me that the lion may be surviving on fish and waterfowl at the river. I never thought of that food source for them.

At Fraile I set my tent in the same place I did last time, in the lee of the roche moutonnée, and begin cooking pasta. Antonio, El Polaco Loco, comes into the camp with three Argentinean girls in tow. No wonder I haven't been able to find him. He comes over to say hello and give excuses. He's going to attempt to take the girls on the glacier. I'm somewhat entertained, especially that he is carrying everyone's crampons and tents, but disappointed in his character. I thought he was a friend. I thought we were partners on the trip to Paso Marconi. At least he could have left a note at my tent. But that's all his problem, not mine, so I remember to be compassionate, and treat him well, but make it clear that I'm not happy that he disappeared with no communication. As I see it, this will help him to gain integrity in the future. I wish him good luck, and they continue upriver to camp at the terminal lake.

After my belly-full I go searching for the trail I will need in the morning. I can't find it, so I ask the horse packer who's putting horses in a tiny barn for the night. He walks me out and shows me a faint trail in the pasture, which I follow easily, as it grows more obvious with distance from the horses. When it hits the toe of the slope of the valley wall, I return to camp and hit the sack.

The clock reads 4:58 when I wake before the alarm. Outside the stars are moving faster than the wind, and it's dead quiet above the blanket of cold dew. I'm packed and on the trail in just a few minutes. At the toe of the valley wall I look up the steep ascent to see

the Southern Cross blazing just over its horizon, and take my first step up. Every step after that is up, crossing tundra, then sharp talus. After an hour there's enough light to turn off my headlight. After two hours I'm at a high, mostly frozen tarn dammed by a tiny moraine, and allowing views of El Chaltén. While ascending from there the first rays strike the summit and I go to work, but I'm not thrilled with the compositions, so I continue up at a fast pace, even though Fitz gets obscured by the massive granite block I pass below. This thing must give the pass its name. It's the size of a big city office building. The

2008

traverse below it is a steep and rock-solid snowfield. A slip could be serious, especially because I'm using my staff instead of an ice axe. So I step slowly, digging my boot edges into the crust. Just before the pass, the giant comes back into view, framed by the big block on the left, and the jagged stegosaurus ridge of the pass on the right. The framing is perfect, and I wonder if this is the reason it's called Paso Cuadrado. "Cuadrado" literally means "square" but it could refer to the block of stone or the square-framed view. It must be the huge block. Most people wouldn't notice the framed view. While I maneuver around ice and rock seeking the best composition, one leg breaks through a snow bridge hiding a small crevasse, and my leg goes in up to my crotch and swings freely in the air below—a warning to be careful.

As I attain the col, an alpine fairyland is revealed. The views are immense and imposing. El Chaltén looms above to the left. Cerro Torre and its neighboring up-valley needles are spread before me, and the Great Southern Icefield stretches beyond into Chile, where Cerro Gorra Blanca—"White Cap"—floats in a sea of white several days' travel from here. No wind blows, only the thunder of avalanches, distant and done, find my ear. I score dozens of photos including several sets of panoramas and a 360 degree panning video.

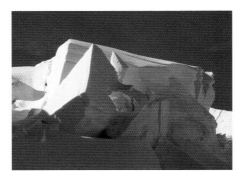

"Valhalla" is the name I give the icefield near my Alaska home, and this view has the same feeling—that of the realm of the mountain gods. It is a crystalline world, pure, seemingly free of biology. If my memory is correct, the Tibetans referred to this kind of environment as the realm of wisdom because of these qualities.

The Patagonian Wind

I'm nestled behind a big boulder on the south slope of Laguna Torre, just above the terminus of the glacier. The sun is shining on me, but I'm holed-up in the lee of this rock

2006

where I'm sheltered from the horizontal rain riding on the relentless wind. I'm hoping the weather will clear, but up the valley, Cerro Torre looks pretty nasty, with an inky dark cloud

covering the peak and a veil of rain screening the shaded ramparts below.

The wind is violent out on the glacier, and I'm hesitant to travel up the ice as I intended. Already I've been blown off balance a few times. Out on the open ice the wind will be worse, and if it doesn't let up, it will be an Aeolian nightmare to endure for no reason.

I intended to travel up the ice, into the glaciered valley between Cerro Torre and El Chaltén, to get views of the tower from below and from the north. It looks like I'll have to throw in the towel. Too bad. We only had two days of good weather instead of the four that El Polaco Loco thought we would have. Now he's stuck somewhere up on the glacier in this weather with the three inexperienced girls. One might fantasize that this is a good thing, but I'm sure the reality is otherwise.

I burnt up the two days—the first I descended from Paso Cuadrado and went back to town, this time catching a ride in a remis (a kind of taxi) that came to pick up a Brazilian couple who were on a day hike. I had promised Evelyn I'd return for her goodbye party, and ended up having another late night with the Argentineans. So the second day I lollygagged with Evelyn drinking maté all morning, watching rufous-necked sparrows (or *chingolos*) hop around camp, and telling stories about the redwoods, skiing the back country behind my cabin in Alaska, and about surfing the waves of the Northern California winter. I was hanging out with her because she'd be leaving on the next morning's bus. Work was slowing down, and she's been camped here for over four months, so she's ready to make tracks. In the short time we've spent together we've become good friends. It was noon by the time I went to rent crampons and finally got on the trail to Laguna Torre.

I spent the few hours on the trail learning how to walk. Twenty years ago I was studying human movement and how it is influenced by chronic holding patterns in the muscles as well as habituated misuse and nonuse of muscles. I was fascinated with the psychological origins of many of these patterns, and became particularly interested in the walking gait and explored it. At the same time I was attending Buddhist meditation retreats and spending several long days alternating between walking and sitting meditation. I sought a

natural, relaxed gait, discovered it and analyzed the three-dimensional undulations that are expressed in the spine and hips of a relaxed person taking steps. I thought I knew how to walk. I like it, and I'm a fast hiker. But I just came to the full realization that I don't engage my gluteus muscles as I should, especially when climbing hills. I say "full" realization because now it seems that I have known this for four or five years. How does it happen that you know something for a few years and then realize it?

A few days ago Antonio, El Polaco Loco, told me that his butt was sore from hiking up to the first view-point on the trail to El Chaltén. He'd been sedentary for over a week and had gotten out of shape. The thought passed through my head that the soreness was from using the gluteus maximus to hike uphill. I've never had that soreness. Today I paid attention and changed my uphill gate to engage that muscle. To do so I have to pay attention to each step.

When I was a teenage oarsman I developed strong quadriceps. The front of my thighs were heavily muscled, while the hamstrings behind were neglected. I developed an extreme imbalance of musculature that I'm only now realizing the consequences of. I came to rely on those strong quadriceps to do more that they ought to, and I called on them to push me uphill. It's another version of "your strength becomes your weakness," one of my often-used maxims. Today I shifted my weight towards my heel and worked on drawing my heel back, rather than pushing forward from my toes. The latter is well-known and comfortable—relying on my strength. The former is strange. It makes me feel like the poor farmers in Japanese samurai movies who always run around with a tight ass. Maybe I'll get used to it. I hope so. It'll prevent musculoskeletal problems as I age.

About three-quarters of the way to the laguna, just after I saw an American kestrel, I noticed that the toe of my right sole had delaminated from the boot. I initiated a search for boot glue, first visiting all the guide camps, then taking the crest of the terminal moraine at the edge of the laguna—a lake with one of the most spectacular views of any lake in the world—to the backpackers camp, and hitting everyone in it for something to stick my sole back on my boot. No glue, but Marius, an Afrikaner from South Africa, gave me dental floss and a strong needle, which I worked with while sitting on a sun-warmed boulder at the edge of the lake, watching the sky back-light the spire at sunset while a *remolinera comun* hopped around the waterline. I protected the threads with duct tape, and

2008

all is functional now. After finishing the job I returned the repair materials and hung out with Marius and his wife Genie—people that I felt comfortable with right away. Marius said he thinks travel is essential to mental health—because it breaks people out of the world-view they create and solidify for themselves just by living in one place, talking to the same people, reading the same newspaper, watching the same TV. He said it's easy to fall into a rut. I said that it's guaranteed, it's human nature.

They invited me to come visit them in Africa, and I accepted. Marius decided to join me at the lake for sunrise, but when we woke it was warm and there were no stars. I went to the lake anyway, and Marius joined me, in case the sun's rays wiggled through a hole in the clouds and lit the peak for a minute. They did. A rosy patch swept the walls of the purple tower for a minute. Three condors spiraled overhead.

After breakfast they headed to El Chaltén and I went to the Tyrollean traverse and crossed the river as I did before, but this time with my backpack hanging from the taut line

by a carabiner in front of me. My legs wrapped around my pack and kept it with me as I laid back and reached behind hand over hand to pull myself across. On the trail up the crest of the lateral moraine the weather began to worsen. I was blown off the trail a few times. The route climbs high into a lenga forest in order to skirt cliffs and landslides. In the forest I was protected. So were the thorn-tailed rayaditos—little chickadee-like birds with long, spiky tail-feathers. When I exited the forest I was ambushed by an aggressive wind wielding big raindrops. A couple of guides were there with a group of disappointed clients. They told me the barometric pressure was dropping. I only went a few hundred yards before taking shelter behind this tall rock, and putting on rain gear.

The guides took the paying customers down to the ice, but I decided it's not my idea of a good time to go down, see how bad it is, and climb back up with my full pack. Any hopes for a photograph are too slim, so I'm enjoying the shelter, the ham and cheese sand-

2008

wiches, and Conrad Herwig playing "The Latin Side of John Coltrane" on my iPod. Every once-in-a-while I walk around the rock, get blasted by the ongoing gale, and verify that the peak is burdened by heavy clouds. I can't talk myself into continuing. It could easily worsen and be sheer hell on the ice all night in tent-wrecking gusts. But it's hard to quit, and it's comfortable behind this boulder, so I'm waiting for a sign of improvement.

Again I try to understand the powerful effect these big rocks can have on the human mind. It's as if they can show us the truth, if we are willing to see, just as a saint speaks the truth if we are willing to listen. Maybe, just as few saints walk among humans, Nature creates a few wonders on the planet during any epoch to help us realize the sacred quality of this existence on the physical plane. Who knows, maybe these granite avatars stand here to help human consciousness evolve.

While hiking the trail to town I see lots of heumul tracks. Huemul are a large deer that locals call *La Fantasma de Patagonia*—"The Ghost of Patagonia"—because they are so rarely seen. By the time I make the streets, the wind is nasty. I'm tired of it. I pass by Fernando's internet lounge and stop in for a visit. Evelyn had brought my street gear here as she promised she would, and I grab it out of his back room. I tell him I want to leave on the morning bus for El Calafate so I can cross the border and see Torres del Paine National Park in Chile. When I complain to Fernando about the wind, he tells me that the wind is why everyone in town wears a wool hat over their ears—not to keep warm, but to keep the wind out of their ears. Then he offers the use of a small cabin he owns, and I thankfully accept.

On my way across town to the cabin, I see Jesus. He is one of the many high-profile local characters I've met in my travels—extraverted loners who don't fit socially-accepted

2008

norms. Like many others, Jesus is friendly. He camps at Madsen and knows me because he's passed my tent a dozen times while I'm sitting on the grass. He always says hello to me now, even from a distance. Like a Rasta named Goat who camped on a Caribbean beach near me in 1982, and used to yell to me every time he saw me, Jesus always sends me a cheerful greeting. He is a hard-working man, finding manual labor on days when there's no work for him as a porter. His face is young but weather-wrinkled around his narrow-set eyes and large nose. A long ponytail leaves the back of his black beret. He's always on a mission when I see him in town.

Later, when I return to have a final dinner with Fernando, he answers my questions and tells stories. He says that the town of El Chaltén exists because the government subsidizes the utilities, making gas and electricity cheaper than it should be. Otherwise the people could not survive the long winter. He says that in order to buy land here you have to live in the town for three years—that is, unless you have connections; after all, it is South America. They are just building a firehouse this year. Usually when there's a house on fire, phone calls race around town and everyone shows up, but there's nothing they can do, so they just watch it burn.

When he asks, I tell him stories about my life, and he admits he is envious. He loves to travel, and was about to take off for Spain when the Argentinean peso crashed. All of a sudden his ten-thousand-dollar savings was worth three-thousand, and he couldn't afford to go. The economy is recovering slowly. He doesn't know when he'll be able to travel again, but he wants to come to Alaska. I wonder if he'll ever make it; I wonder how it would feel to earn pesos that can't compete with most of the developed world.

I fight the wind back to the cabin at a reasonable hour. It howls by the walls all night, and into the morning, when I lay out my gear and get organized and packed—a task that would have been unpleasant if I was camping, or even a guest in a hostel dormitory. When I venture out to buy a ticket for a bus to El Calafate, the town seems empty—a ghost town belted by the strange combination of dust and rain, both riding on hit-and-run gusts racing down from the mountains—the dust made by the merciless pressure of ice on rock, and kicked up from the street of glacial cobble, the rain made by the merciless pressure of wind on mountains that force it up where it expands and sheds its moisture, and the odd spray rides the williwaw down to town.

If Argentina hadn't created the town of El Chaltén to establish a presence near a disputed border with Chile, if the Argentinean Peso wasn't devalued to a third of its worth,

and if international travel hadn't become so common, it would still be only a very few explorers who would make the arduous pilgrimage to this sacred range. But now the village is a destination on the Patagonian travel circuit, and thousands of pilgrims witness the magnificence of these towers every year. In my heart I feel it may be all by some divine plan to hasten the spiritual evolution of our species. But then again, my brain says maybe it's just a series of flukes that cascade to create the present circumstance, where people take a vacation and come to see big rocks and say, "Wow," and occasionally one romantic is so stunned as to conclude that some Divine Intelligence is behind it all.

There's really no way to know for sure if these are granite avatars—no way to prove anything—but I can feel it in my heart. If the rock shows me the divinity and sacredness of Nature, then for me it is an avatar. Now I know that Nature its divine. Funny, seems like I've always known it, but now I fully realize it. Maybe it was just an argument between my heart and my mind, and my heart finally won.

"Because the world is seen, we have to infer a common cause (a Lord) possessing unlimited powers to appear as the diversity. The pictures consisting of names and forms, the seer, the canvas, the light – all these are He Himself."

—Ramana Maharshi (*Forty Verses*)

2008

"What is beauty? It isn't a sensual question, nor a sexual question. It is a very serious question because, without beauty in your heart, you cannot flower in goodness. Have you ever looked at a mountain or the blue sea without chattering, without making noise, really paying attention to the blue sea, the beauty of light on a sheet of water? When you see the extraordinary beauty of the earth, its rivers, lakes, mountains, what actually takes place? What takes place when you look at something which is actually marvelously beautiful: a statue, a poem, a lily in a pond, or a well-kept lawn? At that moment, the very majesty of a mountain makes you forget yourself. Have you ever been in that position?

"If you have, you have seen that then you don't exist, only that grandeur exists. But a few seconds later or a minute later, the whole cycle begins, the confusion, the chatter. So beauty is, where you are not."

—J Krishnamurti

(speaking in Mumbai, India, 1982)

2008

Epilogue

My first visit to El Chaltén was in January of 2006, when I backpacked into these magical mountains, camping at Laguna Torre, Poincenot, and Fraile. I was lucky to return with some good photographs and my teacher, Dr. Shozo Sato, encouraged me to consider creating a collection of them in book form, so I returned the next year. It was on this second visit, in March of 2007, that I made the other backpacking trips in this book. I then proceeded to Chile's Torres del Paine national park, where I lost my camera and 600 photos. So I returned a third time, in January of 2008, with dogged determination to get the photographs I needed.

By 2008 the town of El Chaltén had about doubled in size and the road to it from El Calafate had mostly been paved. Fernando not only offered high-speed internet, but was providing Wi-Fi to the entire town by the time I left. On that third trip I accompanied Waldo and his climbing partner, Indio, to Paso Superior, where we dug a snow cave and spent two nights. Their attempt to climb Poincenot was unsuccessful (due to high winds), but I was able to photograph Monte Fitz Roy (El Chaltén) from the high pass. I also succeeded in a solo ascent of Glaciar Torre to the base-camp for climbing Cerro Torre, "Nipo Nino."

As this book goes to press, an e-mail from Evelyn tells me that Madsen free camp has been closed.

"The love that you search for everywhere is already present within you. It may be evoked by any number of people or events. A mountain can evoke this love. A sunset can evoke this love. But finally, you must realize you are this love. The source of all love is within you."

—Gangaji

2008

Index to the Photographs